Holiness and Human Nature

Holiness
and
Human Nature

by

Leon and Mildred Chambers

Beacon Hill Press of Kansas City
Kansas City, Missouri

First Printing, 1975

Revised from an earlier volume,
Human Nature and Perfecting Holiness
Copyright, 1972

Printed in the United States of America

ISBN: 0-8341-0381-8

Contents

Foreword

Theological insight and thorough psychological training are as yet a rare combination among us. Dr. and Mrs. Leon Chambers possess both in large measure.

Leon and Mildred Chambers are graduates of Trevecca Nazarene College. Rev. Chambers also graduated from Nazarene Theological Seminary and is an ordained minister on the Alabama District. Both have earned doctor's degrees: Mr. Chambers, Ed.D., University of Southern Mississippi; and Mrs. Chambers, Ph.D., George Peabody College for Teachers.

Holiness and Human Nature deals with an area we have often "swept under the rug." While we have long known that "we have this treasure in earthen vessels" (2 Cor. 4:7), we have not always thought through its practical implications. Either the value of the treasure has been emphasized to the extent that the vessels containing it were thought to be practically glorified, or the chips and cracks in the vessels have been used to minimize the treasure.

With courage and insight, the authors deal with problems that arise in the area where the divine ideal and human reality converge. They are clear and unhedging in respect to the divine ideal. They are honest and forthright in their evaluation of the human reality.

Authors often read the books of others they would themselves like to have written. This is such a book for me.

—W. T. PURKISER

Chapter 1

Perfecting Earthen Vessels

Perfect holiness was God's intention from the beginning. Man was created in the image of a holy God. "So God created man in his own image, in the image of God created he him; male and female created he them" (Gen. 1:27). The tragedy is that man did not retain God's image. Eve "took of the fruit thereof, and did eat, and gave also unto her husband with her; and he did eat" (Gen. 3:6).

The effect of the Fall extended to the whole race. "And Adam lived an hundred and thirty years, and begat a son in his own likeness, after his image; and called his name Seth" (Gen. 5:3). Not only had Adam and Eve lost the divine image, but there was a racial loss. The likeness of God had been corrupted by sin. All that man now possessed was the corrupted nature of Adam. This is not a nature for which we bear guilt; it is an inherited nature for which we are unfortunate. It is not a nature needing forgiveness; it is a nature that needs cleansing. A purification from this sinful nature is promised to all. "And God, which knoweth the hearts, bare them witness, giving them the Holy Ghost, even as he did unto us; and put no difference between us and them, purifying their hearts by faith" (Acts 15:8-9).

Not only may we be purified, but John tells how we may remain free from sin. "But if we walk in the light, as

7

he is in the light, we have fellowship one with another, and the blood of Jesus Christ his Son cleanseth us from all sin" (1 John 1:7). The truth is simple. God the Holy Spirit will purify the heart in response to faith, and the person can remain cleansed from all sin by walking in the light.

Redemption from all sin is the purpose of God. "And she shall bring forth a son, and thou shalt call his name JESUS: for he shall save his people from their sins" (Matt. 1:21). "This is a faithful saying, and worthy of all acceptation, that Christ Jesus came into the world to save sinners; of whom I am chief" (1 Tim. 1:15).

Salvation, then, is from all sin. There is no promise that God will take away any of our normal human nature. We are what we are because of genetic inheritance and what we have learned. Salvation from sin does not change one's genetic inheritance nor erase what he has learned. Man and nature still suffer from the Fall.

These frailties in man—mental and physical—are referred to as "infirmities." They are not sinful. God's promise is that He will help us with these frailties. "Likewise the Spirit also helpeth our infirmities . . ." (Rom. 8: 26). There is no promise of deliverance from our infirmities until the day of glorification.

Paul was very conscious of a deliverance yet to come when he wrote, "If by any means I might attain unto the resurrection of the dead. Not as though I had already attained, either were already perfect: but I follow after, if that I may apprehend that for which also I am apprehended of Christ Jesus" (Phil. 3:11-12).

Until the resurrection we will struggle with our infirmities, helped by the Holy Spirit. It is the purpose of this book to differentiate between these infirmities and sin, so that one may not feel guilty for infirmities but, with courage, work toward maturity of his human nature for the glory of God. Salvation is from all sin by the grace of God, but cooperating with the workings of the Holy Spirit in these earthen vessels is a responsibility of the Christian: "Let us cleanse ourselves from all filthiness of the flesh and spirit, perfecting holiness in the fear of God" (2 Cor. 7:1).

Chapter 2

Holiness and Human Nature

Some would make the experience of sanctification mean too little. Others, however, would insist upon a perfection that would rob man of his humanity. It is the thesis of this book that the experiences of conversion and sanctification deal with the sin problem in the human life and do not eradicate any of man's basic humanity. The Holy Spirit helps us with human weaknesses or infirmities; He does not eliminate them.

Let us consider some of the areas where there tend to be misunderstandings relative to the work of the Holy Spirit and human nature.

ERRING IN JUDGMENT

The experience of holiness does not mean that one will not err in judgment. The perfection required is perfection of motives, not perfection of the intellect. In Acts 11 the apostles and brethren "contended" (that is, "differed") with Peter over his eating with the Gentiles. Peter explained that he was directed by a revelation from God to eat, preach, and pray with the Gentiles and the same apostles and brethren "glorified God, saying, Then hath God also to the Gentiles granted repentance unto life" (v. 18). The brethren erred, but they had not sinned. Their contention would have hindered the Church, but there was no rebellion against the known will of God. When light came, they walked in it.

Such obedience keeps one sinless and guiltless even when there are errors in judgment that result in misunderstanding. These errors may be stumbling blocks to the one who errs and to others as well. It is possible that they could even keep some unsaved person out of the Kingdom. But there is no sin or guilt in mistakes and errors in judgment. As long as one is not rebellious, is walking in the light and obedient, he is a fully accepted child of God.

To say that the Christian who errs in judgment has not sinned is not to say that he may be indifferent and will not need to improve. He will lament, grieve, and pray over his errors. While they are not held against him as sins, they will prevent his being as effective a Christian as he might be and will certainly affect the rewards of eternity.

LACK OF HARMONY AMONG THE SPIRIT-FILLED

The experience of holiness does not mean that there will always be perfect harmony among the Spirit-filled. Paul and Barnabas, accompanied by Mark, were "sent forth by the Holy Ghost" on the first missionary journey (Acts 13:4). Later, however, Paul refused to take Mark on a second missionary journey. "And the contention was so sharp between them, that they departed asunder one from the other" (Acts 15:39). The words *departed asunder* in the Greek New Testament mean "a violent division, forcible separation."

The division was not sin; it was human. There is no evidence of any unkind, ulterior motives. In fact, when Mark later proved himself, Paul wrote, "Only Luke is with me. Take Mark, and bring him with thee: for he is profitable to me for the ministry" (2 Tim. 4:11). Paul did not let differences cut him off from fellowship. The Bible plainly says there were strong differences, but there was a willingness to change with additional light on the subject. When Mark proved himself worthy as a missionary, Paul received him with open arms.

Paul and Barnabas felt strong emotion. Each believed that he was right. There is no sin in experiencing differences if the motive of love is present. The spirits of Paul and Barnabas were such that God was able to use two missionary parties instead of one. God was able to use a misunderstanding for His glory. He was able to place His blessings upon Paul through the guidance of the Holy Spirit (Acts 16:6). Even though the second missionary journey began with a division among the missionaries, their attitudes were not those of revenge, unrighteousness, or hatred; and God was able to use both missionary groups.

There is no sin in misunderstandings and differences of opinions. There *may* be sin in one's attitude concerning them.

LACK OF PHYSICAL PERFECTION

Holiness does not insure physical perfection. During Christ's agony in the garden, fatigued disciples fell asleep. When Jesus returned from prayer, He admonished Peter, "What, could ye not watch with me one hour?" (Matt. 26:40). This incident shows physical weakness on the part of the disciples, but certainly no one would accuse them of having sinned.

Records of suffering saints and accounts of prayers for healing that go unanswered fill the pages of Christian literature. Spiritual warriors sometimes seem to fall early in the warfare against the enemy. Dedicated men and women weep because physical limitations keep them from achieving for God as they wish they could.

Paul experienced such a problem. "And lest I should be exalted above measure through the abundance of the revelations, there was given to me a thorn in the flesh, the messenger of Satan to buffet me, lest I should be exalted above measure. For this thing I besought the Lord thrice, that it might depart from me. And he said unto me, My grace is sufficient for thee: for my strength is made perfect in weakness" (2 Cor. 12:7-9). God did not deliver Paul from his physical problem, but He did promise grace to bear it. God also said that He would be glorified as Paul bore his weakness.

The sanctified person has a body that shows the effects of the Fall. This body tires, falls prey to diseases, at times functions with difficulty. It may take great physical effort to carry on one's work for the Lord. The fact that special effort is required is not a sin. One need not feel guilty. God understands our humanity. Sanctification does not give an extra supply of energy; it does not make a person superhuman.

There are Christians who will live all their lives and come to the time of death praying for deliverance from physical burdens, but God will not deliver. The Bible teaches that God has power to heal, but He does not always heal. Physical imperfections can be suffered by the most dedicated, sanctified child of God.

Lack of Perfection of Works or Discipline

Holiness does not mean perfection of works or self-discipline. The sanctified man will not necessarily give his best each time that he has an opportunity to work for the Lord. Humanity prevents this. In 2 Tim. 1:5, Paul expressed deep appreciation for Timothy's faith: "When I call to remembrance the unfeigned faith that is in thee," Paul is speaking of Timothy's faithfulness to God. But immediately he gives an admonition: "Stir up the gift of God, which is in thee" (v. 6). Even with Timothy's faithfulness, he could improve his service.

Since the infilling with the Holy Spirit does not take away one's humanity, each person must keep his body under the control of the spiritual man. That one comes short and is slack in his work for the Kingdom is not a sin that severs his relationship to God. These shortcomings certainly make us less effective Christians and can lessen our joy in the Lord. They can even lead to backsliding. Yet realization that one has fallen short in his efforts should not place one in a state of despair; it should be, as Paul told Timothy, an occasion for stirring up the gift of God and improving one's service to God. It is human to have shortcomings. But it is Christian to press on, to seek God's grace, and to try to overcome these frailties of humanity.

Subject to Temptation

Holiness does not place one beyond temptation. The brain is like a receiving center for a network of radar screens. From the senses messages are sent to the brain. All experiences are recorded on the cortex of the brain. When there is a stimulus, any of these experiences may be remembered. Learning is not always intentional but may occur spontaneously.

When one is saved, his sins are forgiven. However, the experiences of his sinful life are still recorded on the brain in what are called "memory traces," which are never erased. Scientists have discovered that by the use of electrodes past experiences may be revived with all the

14

reality of reliving them. In everyday living the person will remember past experiences under certain circumstances.

The fact that even after sanctification past sinful experiences may be recalled and be a source of temptation is a strong argument for clean living. If one has created abnormal appetites, these may become the occasion for temptation. At any time, place, or combination of events, if the devil can get one's attention for even a moment, he will use these past experiences as a source of temptation. This is not sin. The devil may even bring thoughts of something that one has never done by using what is called substitute stimulus. This is not sin. It is, however, a good reason to shun the very appearance of evil. But to be tempted is not sin. "For we have not an high priest which cannot be touched with the feeling of our infirmities; but was in all points tempted like as we are, yet without sin" (Heb. 4:15).

If a person's sins are forgiven and his heart is sanctified wholly, memories of the past may be a source of temptation but not sin. The past may be a battleground— a bloody, vicious, bruising battleground—but it does not have to be defeat.

NEGATIVE EMOTIONS

Holiness does not place one beyond the possibility of experiencing negative emotions such as hurt feelings, impatience, worry, anxiety, and similar emotions. To feel an emotion, even strong emotion, is not sin within itself; it is human. One must know the motive behind the emotion to determine its purity or sinfulness. The *motive* is an internal state that is the cause of behavior. Values and goals are products of our motives. Motives determine the behavior involved in reaching a particular goal.

An emotion is an aroused or stirred-up state. Man is

an emotional creature. There is no sin in being emotional. Emotions influence all of one's behavior. They motivate us to action. Note the "—motion" in *emotion*.

Emotions can help us enjoy or dislike a task. They facilitate or impede learning. They influence our interpretation of another person's behavior, either positively or negatively. While unbridled emotions can erode one's spiritual life to the point that they can become sin, they need not do so. We need a well-developed, well-balanced emotional life in order to be normal persons.

Emotions are accompanied by a variety of physical responses which are not under conscious control. The changes involved in an emotional response depend upon the type and intensity of the emotion. Examples of these changes are accelerated heartbeat, accelerated breathing, variation in rate of speech, dryness of mouth, dilation of the pupils of the eyes, sweating, and alterations in brain waves. When there is strong emotion, the organism is in a state of red alert. The release of sugar into the blood, more rapid blood-clotting time, and a general gain in strength make the organism ready for extreme emergencies. In fact, no human or animal could survive without these processes. When there is a stressful stimulus, these physical changes take place automatically.

Many scientists believe that emotions are under the control of the hypothalamus, a small part of the brain just over the roof of the mouth. This little organ sends messages to the adrenal glands. They in turn secrete hormones into the bloodstream. This is not a conscious control, although the adrenals are under the control of the brain. If someone screams, "Fire," one may act and then think later. The small lady who lifted the fallen car off her trapped husband did not have time to think.

People differ in their emotional responses. All people are emotional, but no two are alike. A recognition of individual differences is necessary or we will stumble in our understanding of perfect love. These individual differences are genetically and environmentally based.

People are born with different emotional makeups, dispositions, or temperaments. Scientists now believe that some people inherit a type of nervous system that tends to cause them to react faster and with more intensity than others. Studies of newborn babies show great variability in emotional responses to the same stimuli. Some react violently, others mildly, others hardly at all. Some are pacified easily, some with great difficulty.

The environment of our early years plays an important role in our emotional behavior patterns. People learn ways of responding according to the behavior patterns they find to be rewarding. A child who gets his way by sulking will repeat the behavior because he has been rewarded. Children learn ways of responding from their parents. Cheerful parents tend to foster this quality in their children, while antagonistic parents foster angry children.

Paul seemed to have no problem in preaching to the Gentiles while Peter required a special revelation. Barnabas had no problem in forgiving Mark, while Paul required Mark to prove himself. This would say to us that some people find it easier to forgive and forget than do others. Some people just seem to be nice by nature while others seem to have trouble even with the help of the Holy Spirit.

Just as being saved and sanctified does not heal all physical ailments, these experiences do not solve all psychological problems. One's genetic inheritance and social background are still there even when one is saved and sanctified.

Since people differ so greatly in emotional responses and since emotions can be evaluated only on the basis of the underlying motives, we would do well to judge no

17

man. To get "red in the face" cannot be equated with hostile motives, as is so often thought. A person might react quickly, speak sharply, and even flush; but these responses may be the result of humiliation, threat to security, fear, or embarrassment, as well as anger. There is little biological difference between the emotions of fear and anger. Another person might become pale in response to the same stimulus. Only the true Judge of motives can classify. No human is capable of judging. "Judge not" was given with good reason (Matt. 7:1).

The sanctified may even experience strong emotions. Jesus experienced some kind of strong emotion in Gethsemane. Luke 22:44 speaks of Christ as "being in an agony." The original Greek shows the word *agony* to mean "a conflict or struggle." The agony referred to was mental. It was more than mere physical pain. The mental aspect is implied in "conflict" and "struggle." We cannot classify the emotion specifically, but it obviously was strong emotion. Otherwise, it would not have affected the physical body as it did. In the same verse Luke said, ". . . and his sweat was as it were great drops of blood falling down to the ground."

Whether a strong emotion is sinful depends upon what occasioned it and how it is handled. It must be kept in mind, also, that emotions may lead to sin if they result in loss of faith in God until the motive life is affected to the point of rebelling against God.

Gal. 2:11 implies that Paul experienced strong emotions toward Peter: "But when Peter was come to Antioch, I *withstood* him to the face, because he was to be blamed." From the Greek New Testament the word *withstood* means "to set oneself against, to withstand, resist, or oppose." Paul's emotions were aroused because Peter dissembled against the Gentiles by refusing to eat with them, and he influenced other Jews, including Barnabas, to do the same. Paul withstood Peter "before them all" (Gal. 2:14).

The sanctified may experience the emotions of anxiety, worry, impatience, discontent, and related emotions. At the outset it might be well to point out that often disagreement concerning emotions is a problem of semantics. For example, what one person would call "concern," another would call "worry." Someone else may use the term *anxiety* for the same emotional response. The term *mad* is used very loosely, as is the term *angry.* This once again points out the problem of classifying and judging another's emotions.

In Luke 10:40, Martha is described as apparently experiencing one or more of the emotions of worry, impatience, discontent, or anxiety: "But Martha was cumbered about much serving, and came to him, and said, Lord, dost thou not care that my sister hath left me to serve alone? bid her therefore that she help me." While Jesus did not condone, neither did He rebuke as He would have had He classified her behavior as sinful.

Let us take a look at some specific emotions.

1. *Concern.* Concern may be defined as caring about or regarding something. It is considered a somewhat mild emotion. Everyone would agree as to the place of concern in daily living. Christ in His parable of the unjust steward recognized the legitimate place of concern. The unjust steward was commended and told that those who are concerned and plan for the future are wise (Luke 16:1-8).

2. *Worry.* Worry is considered by many authorities to be a mild response to fear. Worry is a common emotion, closely related to anxiety but more mild. This emotion is characterized by a circular thought pattern. The worrier in his preoccupation with his problem thinks over the problem again and again, which may be called circular

thinking. Worrying breeds more worry. Fear provokes worry, and worry provokes more fear.

Worry is a nonconstructive, nonadjustive response. Worry can have detrimental physical effects. The chronic worrier may literally worry himself thin or sick. Worry may lead to severe anxiety reactions.

As with other emotional reactions, worry may spring from one's environmental background. One may have developed a worry habit reaction because of experiences in an anxiety-ridden home. The worry pattern developed was an attempt to adjust to the constant anxiety.

Worry in itself is not sin. Paul was so disturbed (worried) concerning the state of the church at Thessalonica that he could not rest until Timothy was sent to investigate and returned with a good report. Paul said, "I could no longer forbear" (1 Thess. 3:5).

Worry may result from the guilt one feels because of sins committed. But for the Christian whose sins are forgiven the fears that underlie his worry are not based upon guilt for sins committed; therefore the worry is not sin.

Death is our enemy. It is normal to fear death. A sanctified man may be told that he has a terminal illness. He might go through a period of preoccupation with this problem based upon fear. He might be said to "worry" about the condition. He has not sinned. Naturally, in proportion to the degree that one is able to rise above the fear, worry diminishes.

Again, individuals differ. There are those who because of genetic disposition and poor social and religious backgrounds may not have the ability to make the adjustment to fear situations that another person could make.

3. *Anxiety.* Anxiety is a strong emotion of apprehension or uneasiness stemming from threat or danger, the source of which may be unidentifiable. In this sense it

differs from fear in that the latter is attached to an identifiable object or event in the environment. As with any aroused state, the physiology of the body is altered, the extent of alteration depending upon the degree of anxiety. It is a more intense emotion than either of the foregoing.

For example, the nerves may be so reactive as to be "on edge," causing one to respond out of proportion to the stimulus. He may jump at the slightest noise. The heart and the breathing rate may accelerate; digestion may slow down or speed up; and even the skin may respond with flushing, pallor, or sweating. All these are automatic reactions when we feel threatened, as in anxiety.

Our age is sometimes called the "Age of Anxiety" because of the many threats to normal daily living and even to survival. Sanctified people experience threats to physical well-being and will respond biologically with automatic responses. The nervous system is made in such a way that the emotion of anxiety is a natural response to threat.

Jesus probably experienced some form of anxiety when He actually faced "the cup." As we have seen, His physiological reaction was sweating "as it were great drops of blood" (Luke 22:44). Yet Christ did not sin. Once again, sin involves rebellion. A sanctified person who feels threatened may respond with anxiety but without sin.

The term *anxious* is closely related to *anxiety,* both being attached to a future event. The emotion of being anxious is usually considered to be more mild than anxiety. Anxiousness may cause anxiety.

It might be well to look at Matt. 6:31, which reads, "Therefore take no thought, saying, What shall we eat? or, What shall we drink? or, Wherewithal shall we be clothed?" This verse is sometimes rendered, "Be not therefore anxious." Many competent Greek scholars teach the literal meaning to be that we are to "avoid cares that distract, divide the mind, or that draw us in a different direction." Certainly prudent care was not forbidden by our Lord. Jesus is admonishing His listeners to be different from the heathen and the hypocrites, who are overly concerned with the cares of this life.

4. *Impatience.* The sanctified may experience impatience. Impatience is the lack of endurance or long-suffering. One's patience threshold is affected by fatigue, illness, stress, or pressure. In these states, one responds more quickly, is more sensitive to a greater variety of provocations, has less emotional control. A sick or tired person is not a normal person. Even though sanctified, his physical endurance and, specifically, his nervous endurance are limited.

If impatience is a sin, any degree of the emotion is a sin, even impatience with oneself, which all sanctified have experienced even if under some other label. Some would seem to think it is all right to be impatient with oneself, but not with others. This is inconsistent. Impatience within itself is not a sin.

Even Jesus grew weary of faithlessness and expressed it strongly: "O faithless and perverse generation, how long shall I be with you?" (Matt. 17:17). Long-suffering is a fruit of the Spirit. All the Spirit-filled have the fruit of the Spirit, but not all Christians bear all of the fruit equally. There are degrees of spiritual maturity among the sanctified.

5. *Discontentment.* The sanctified may suffer discontentment. This emotion may be constructive in that it may move us to higher levels of action. On the other hand, it may be detrimental when we become preoccupied and can't see beyond our circumstances.

The opposite of discontentment is contentment. Paul said, "For I have learned, in whatsoever state I am, therewith to be content" (Phil. 4:11). Note the word *learned.* Contentment does not come automatically with sanctification—that is, not constant contentment with all things. While discontent within itself is not a sin, the sanctified should learn contentment. "But godliness with contentment is great gain" (1 Tim. 6:6).

The foregoing discussion of emotions has tried to show the place of such common emotions as anxiety, worry, impatience, and other emotions in the life of the sanctified. The purpose is not to "whittle out" a loophole to let one crawl through, settle down, and enjoy and indulge such emotions. The purpose is to help the sanctified avoid self-condemnation for normal, human conduct. Such condemnation can be detrimental to one's spiritual victory.

Remember, one has not sinned as long as his motives are pure and there is no rebellion. Any behavior is sin that is an outgrowth of a sinful motive, whether it be an outward act or an internal emotion. But where the motive is pure, the behavior, whether an outward act or an internal emotion, is not sin.

Certainly, emotions may lead to sin. If the emotion affects the Christian's faith to the point that he becomes rebellious, then his motive is no longer pure. Our goals are set according to our motives. When a motive becomes sinful, then sinful goals will be chosen. Sinful motives and sinful goals result in sinful acts. Thus, emotions may lead to sin.

For example, Martha wanted Jesus to rebuke Mary in order to get her assistance when she was "cumbered" with her household tasks. Jesus did not treat Martha's action as a sin. If Martha had indulged her emotions to the point that she wanted Mary humiliated and embarrassed, then Martha's motives would have been changed, her goal would have changed, and Martha would have been guilty

23

of sin. Her emotions would have been based upon sinful motives and, as such, would have been classified as sinful.

Even when emotions are not sin, they can hinder one's fruitfulness and can be a stumbling block to oneself and others. Peter's emotion of fear of the Jews, which separated him from the Gentiles, made him a stumbling block to the Gentiles. They must have wondered why he ate with them one day and would not eat with them the next. But the fear was not sin.

Sanctification does not change the biology of the nervous system, which is basically responsible for the physical aspects of emotions; but sanctification does purify the motive life. Sanctification will help one to see that he needs to strive to develop the emotional control that is possible within the limits of his physical body.

The experience of holiness does not prevent one from experiencing strong feeling, but it will save one from being unkind or trying to hurt or get even. Holiness will not keep one from desiring fair play, but it will enable him to carry on even if he does not receive fair play. The sanctified person may at times experience hurt, embarrassment, humiliation, or similar emotions; but, by the help of the Holy Spirit, he will walk in the light, return good for evil, and serve God with all his heart.

The question that one might well ask is whether he really loves God with all his heart and loves his fellowman as himself. If he can honestly answer yes, then he need feel no condemnation. There is a place for wide variety of emotions in the life of the sanctified, but there is no place for hatred, revenge, or unkindness.

Lack of Instant Maturity

Holiness does not bring instant maturity. The term *maturation* is used by psychologists and biologists to refer

24

to all the changes that occur between conception and adulthood. These changes are patterned by heredity but require the right environment for development.

The human organism comes into the world helpless. Even so, the infant is a person just as much as the adult is a person. There is, however, much growing to take place. Maturation cannot be rushed or hurried. Even small acts cannot be carried out until nature brings one to the point of readiness. Until the necessary muscular and nervous structures have matured, the organism cannot sit alone, walk, talk, or learn. Even when maturity brings one to the point of readiness to learn, there is an indispensable need for a stimulating, enriching environment to give the opportunity to learn. The child does not learn in a vacuum.

When a person is saved and sanctified, he is just as much a Christian as the one who is mature in Christ. But he is still an infant in Christ. His experience of grace gives him the spiritual basis for growth, just as heredity gives potential for physical growth. But just as an infant needs the right biological environment to develop physically, the infant in Christ needs the right spiritual environment, which includes godly models and the Bread of Life.

Just as an impoverished psychological and biological environment can cause mental retardation, spiritual deprivation may retard a person's spiritual development for all of his earthly existence.

Some psychologists speak of the functionally retarded. These people have all the endowments for a normal life. However, their early experiences were so painful that they later suffer psychological disturbances. Some now believe that, according to the type of experiences during the first four years of one's life, his IQ can be raised or lowered. The functionally retarded, even with the richest of natural endowments, will be only a shadow of what he could have been.

A person may be functionally retarded spiritually. Faulty emotional training, unscriptural beliefs, wrong concepts of faith, the development of an unscriptural conscience, and many other problems may trouble the Christian throughout his earthly journey.

It is vital for the spiritual health of the young Christian that he develop in a rich spiritual environment. The young Christian must know that he is valued for himself, by God and by the church. The mature Christian must be an example in cross-bearing, problem-facing, faith, overt Christian behavior, beliefs, motives, prayer, Bible reading, and Christian discipline.

When one is saved and sanctified, he is only at the beginning. He is now in the spiritual condition to mature. But he must have the right environment. The spiritual infant must be nurtured into the strength of a mature Christian. Just as a child learns values and standards from people who are models (usually the parents), the young Christian learns Christian values and standards from the Christians around him.

Peter gives a description of a young Christian. "As newborn babes, desire the sincere milk of the word, that ye may grow thereby" (1 Pet. 2:2). At the moment of conversion, spiritual learning begins. The infant in Christ, by the help of the Holy Spirit and the church, must shape new behavioral patterns. When this person is filled with the Holy Spirit, there is greater impetus to grow. However, the newly sanctified have only the potential for spiritual growth. The growth is a development of a lifetime. It is not achieved instantaneously.

Just as inherited potential will not be the same for all people, all Christians do not have the same potential. Christians will not be any more alike than the members of a family will be alike.

All Christians do have, however, a set of potentials that are ready to function, some almost immediately and others not for years. Just as the rate of physical maturation is not the same for all children (some walk much earlier than others), the rate of spiritual development will differ among Christians. Just as it is unwise to try to force a child to walk before the muscles and nerves are ready, it is unwise to try to force maturity upon a spiritual infant. No amount of practice, teaching, or coaxing can teach a child to read until he is at a point of readiness where the brain, muscles, and nerves are ready and able. To try to force mature understanding and conduct on a spiritual infant will only produce confusion and frustration.

Let us consider the spiritual environment the church needs to provide for the spiritual infant.

First, the environment must be healthy. The spiritual environment must provide resources for building a mature spiritual adult. The young Christian must feel the love of the Heavenly Father and feel that he is accepted into the church family. This feeling of acceptance needs to be so complete that growth without fear can begin immediately. The spiritual child must know and feel that he is loved for himself.

Second, the environment must offer opportunity for learning. The spiritual infant must learn new ways of responding as old things are left behind. In learning new habits, there will be errors and failures. The new Christian must be so supported by love that he will not reject himself or feel rejected by the church.

Third, the environment must provide reward. There should be a free expression of joy for all progress observed in the young Christian. Just as a child seeks approval of adults, the young Christian needs the approval of mature Christians. Note the beginnings of Paul's letters. He sought to express appreciation for the progress the churches were making before he ever rebuked them.

I stood one day watching my small nephew play in a little plastic swimming pool in his backyard. When Stevie jumped into the water, to show him that I was proud that he wasn't afraid, I clapped my hands. He enjoyed this approval, so he jumped again. I clapped again. He jumped even more vigorously.

When I failed to clap, he said, "Clap, Uncle Leon."

He called my wife and said, "Clap, Aunt Mildred."

Then he called his mother over and asked her to clap. He wanted approval from all of us. He was rewarded by the approval. The water wasn't very deep from the adult viewpoint, but to jump in was an accomplishment for him.

The spiritually immature need the approval of the church, words of encouragement. This will motivate them to conquer greater and greater problems. It encourages maturity. Some psychologists say there is a drive toward mental health. Surely there is a drive toward spiritual maturity, but the right environment is needed.

In the right spiritual environment, the immature Christian can develop at his own rate. This is spiritually healthy. What is a blessing to some will not be a blessing to others. Experiences that will be without difficulty for some will be most difficult for others. No two people feel, see, hear, or experience in exactly the same way. Each person brings all his history into each experience. This makes each activity highly personal. At this point, the church may need to borrow the idea of educators that each person should be encouraged to make progress according to his own personal ability.

For uninhibited spiritual growth each person must feel secure, must respond with Christlike love to others, and his own self-esteem must be enhanced by feeling that others respond to his overtures.

28

One must accept his total Christian life. Where he finds weaknesses, he must seek to improve them. Where he finds strengths, he should rejoice. This may sound simple, but it is a rather difficult task for the young Christian. This is a new life. He needs someone to serve as a standard by which to measure himself. Just as parents are overwhelmed by the needs of their children, adult Christians may be burdened by the excessive and sometimes seemingly unnecessary demands of young Christians. These children in Christ, however, have needs that only mature Christians can meet.

RETENTION OF BIOLOGICAL DRIVES

Holiness does not eradicate biological drives. A majority of the textbooks list hunger, thirst, sleep, and sex among the numerous biological drives. There is no sin in any of these drives. All are necessary for the welfare of the individual and the propagation of the race. There is sin in certain types of behavior in response to the physiological pressures induced by the drives. But there is a Christian way to meet all of the biological drives.

The experiences of being saved and sanctified will not place a person in a state where such drives cannot be stimulated. A drive is only a physiological condition, and this is not sinful. It is only normal and human. The resulting patterns of behavior, however, are of great importance.

Some psychologists teach that there is a strong need for sensory stimulation. Certainly, the organism does seek various kinds of stimuli in relation to its different drives. Again, there is no inherent sin in the organism enjoying the physiological and psychological pleasures of stimulating sensations relating to biological drives. The smell of food may stimulate hunger. The sight of water may stimulate thirst. Any message brought by the senses may stimulate any one or more of the drives. This excited state within itself is not sinful.

There can be, and at times there is, sin related to the drives. Because of this the Bible admonishes the Christian to "abstain from all appearance of evil" (1 Thess. 5:22). "Beloved, follow not that which is evil, but that which is good. He that doeth good is of God: but he that doeth evil hath not seen God" (3 John 11). Sensory stimulation can become intrinsically evil. A person strongly tempted to satisfy any drive in an illicit way is doing evil to expose himself to a condition that serves to satisfy a drive in a sinful way. Biological drives are powerful forces. They are not to be treated carelessly. When drives go unsatisfied, discomfort and tension result which can lead to maddening frustration as well as to sinful conduct.

The sanctified will seek to see, taste, smell, and touch what will be to the glory of God, even though he will be tempted to do otherwise. Sensory stimulation arouses the total organism. The sanctified will not seek to be aroused for evil.

When one considers sensory stimulation, he is dealing with the total motive life and, therefore, with the conduct of the person. It is psychologically impossible to separate the stimuli fed into the organism from the motive life of the person. Sensory stimulation willingly sought is an excellent testimony to what kind of person one is.

While the person sanctified retains his biological drives, he will preserve his vessel in holiness and will seek sensory stimulation only for the advancement of a life of purity. This means that all evil will be shunned and righteousness will be sought. The body will always be kept under submission to the spiritual man. This was Paul's admonition in Rom. 12:1, "Present your bodies a living sacrifice, holy, acceptable unto God, which is your reasonable service." The whole body is on the altar to be used to the glory of God. The drives are not eradicated from the sanctified; they are kept pure.

SELF-LOVE

The experience of sanctification does not bring an end to loving oneself. It has often been preached that one should not love himself. The Bible is very clear that the Christian will love himself. In fact, he cannot be a Bible Christian unless he does love himself. "Thou shalt love thy neighbour as thyself" (Matt. 19:19). The teaching of Jesus is that love for self is the standard for treatment of others.

Psychologists often speak of the self-concept, which is one's image of himself—the way he sees himself in his own private world. The type self-concept developed, whether good or poor, has many implications in the spiritual development and behavior of an individual. The self-concept is learned in early experiences.

A poor self-concept will develop if a child's family reject, tease, or humiliate him—calling him "foolish" or "stupid." The child will grow up to think of himself as unworthy. He will tend to distrust his world, to reject himself. It is hard for a person with a poor self-concept to love himself.

A poor self-concept may also be developed where a child is taught to think too highly of himself. He is in danger of trying tasks that are too demanding for his abilities. This often causes him to suffer inferiority feelings, to be at war with himself and with his world. Because this troubled individual exaggerates his abilities, he experiences failure after failure. He doesn't see himself as he really is. There is a lack of inward harmony. He may put on a front of confidence to the extent that people may think of him as a very poised, self-confident individual when inwardly he may be fearful, uncertain, and self-

31

rejecting. It will also be hard for this individual to love himself.

The basic factors in the development of a good self-concept are feeling loved, accepted, supported, and having opportunity for successful experiences—in short, being in an environment that will cause a person to think well of himself. It will be easier for this person to love himself than for the person with the poor self-concept.

Acceptance of self will largely determine one's attitudes and behavior toward others. The individual with a good self-concept will have reason to be at peace with himself and with others. He feels that he is significant in the sight of God and in his own sight. He has accepted what he can do and what he cannot do. This will bring peace.

The Christian is in the best possible position to love himself and to love others. He can face God without guilt and face himself and others without condemnation. There is no need to strike out at others nor to blame others. Christian love for self is not selfish, not conceited. It is mentally healthy. Christian love is peace with self and with others. A Christian who feels truly loved of God will love himself.

SUMMARY

The experiences of conversion and sanctification solve the sin problem but do not rob man of his basic humanity or eliminate infirmities. God does promise that the Holy Spirit will help us with these human weaknesses. There are several areas where there tends to be misunderstanding relative to the work of the Holy Spirit and human nature.

The sanctified will still err in judgment. Holiness perfects one's motives but not his intellect. His mistakes may be a hindrance to himself and to others, but they are not sin.

A spirit of harmony will not always prevail among the sanctified. So long as misunderstandings and differences of opinion spring from pure motives and do not sever Christian fellowship, there is no sin.

Holiness does not insure physical perfection. The bodies of the sanctified show the effects of the Fall. The Bible and human history attest to physical weaknesses among the saints. While God can heal, He does not always do so.

Holiness does not mean perfection of works or discipline. The sanctified person, hindered by humanity, will not necessarily always give his best to God. He should constantly seek to improve.

The sanctified can be tempted. The brain constantly receives stimuli that Satan may use as a source of temptation. Because sinful experiences of the past are not erased with the infilling of the Holy Spirit, these experiences are used by Satan. To be tempted is not sin.

The sanctified will still experience negative emotions, such as worry, anxiety, and impatience. Emotions can be classified as sin only when the motives are not pure. Even strong emotion is a natural physiological response of the human. People differ in their emotional responses. Because motives can't be seen and because of the differences in emotional responses among people, one should not judge another's emotions as sinful. Emotions may lead to sin when motives become impure and impel one to unchristian behavior. Even when emotions are not sinful, they can hinder a Christian in his personal growth and cause him to be a stumbling block to others. Therefore, with the help of the Holy Spirit, he will strive to improve emotional control and expression.

Holiness does not bring instant maturity. The right spiritual environment helps one to mature faster. An impoverished spiritual environment can cause spiritual retardation. People mature at different rates. Not all Christians have the same potential for maturity.

The biological drives are not eradicated with sanctification. These drives are not sinful but may be the occasion of sinful behavior. Biological drives will be stimulated in the sanctified. He will avoid stimulation that arouses these drives for evil. The drives are not removed from the Spirit-filled, but they are kept pure.

The experience of holiness does not bring an end to self-love. Only as the Christian loves himself can he truly love others.

Chapter 3

The Necessity of Perfecting Holiness

The Bible teaches the necessity of perfecting holiness. In fact, at times the Apostle Paul comes close to placing the responsibility for this solely upon the Christian. "Having therefore these promises, dearly beloved, let us cleanse ourselves from all filthiness of the flesh and spirit, perfecting holiness in the fear of God" (2 Cor. 7:1).

It is therefore as scriptural to perfect the experience as it is to obey the command to seek the experience of entire sanctification. The perfecting of holiness should be the goal of every child of God throughout his earthly journey.

That holiness needs to be perfected does not allow for rebellion or acts of sin in the life of the Christian. The Scriptures are very clear that the children of God do not commit sin. "Whosoever is born of God doth not commit sin; for his seed remaineth in him: and he cannot sin, because he is born of God" (1 John 3:9).

The most dedicated child of God, walking in all of the light God gives, finds himself confessing that his life falls short of what it should be for the greatest glory of the Father. In recognition of these human failings, James exhorts righteous men to confess their faults. "Confess your faults one to another, and pray one for another, that ye may be healed. The effectual fervent prayer of a righteous man availeth much" (Jas. 5:16).

The word *faults* means "offenses, a stumbling or a false step." James calls these "faults," not sins that would bring guilt and separation from God. If one knows he has erred, there should be a frank acknowledgment of the fault. Peace will come through a prayer of confession to God. There will be no joy in hiding, denying, or refusing to admit the stumbling. If there is no rebellion against the known will of God, there is regret but not guilt.

Infirmities, mental and physical weaknesses, are part of human nature. These are not inherently evil. This does not mean that infirmities should be given free rein. They should resolutely be kept under the discipline of a Spirit-controlled will.

We perfect holiness by becoming better Christians. We are still human, but better humans. We will have all the drives, motives, and needs that all men have. There is nothing sinful about being human. It is when sins and the sinful nature take over that human nature becomes obnoxious in the sight of God. God has no design to make angels out of us. He wants to purify us and direct our lives to greater and greater heights each day that we live. He will make it possible to gratify all of our needs in ways that will be to His glory.

When the Christian accepts the scriptural fact that his life will still be burdened with shortcomings, he will find it easier to have mercy on others who fall short. Jesus taught His disciples to pray: "And forgive us our debts, as we forgive our debtors" (Matt. 6:12). Falling short of knowing the perfect will of God constitutes a debt, not a sin. Debts require God's mercy, which is freely given. In the same manner each Christian should forgive himself and others.

An infirmity universally experienced among Christians is inability to quickly and accurately know the will of God. This slowness to comprehend spiritual things is a source of blundering and an occasion for childlike behavior on the part of saints. Because of this, some Christians condemn themselves, burden themselves with remorse, and rob themselves of the peace that they have a right to enjoy. Such an attitude is not the will of God. God gives His way: "Trust in the Lord with all thine heart; and lean not unto thine own understanding. In all thy ways acknowledge him, and he shall direct thy paths" (Prov. 3:5-6). The instantaneous experience of entire sanctification will not solve the problem of knowing God's will. Prayer, growth in grace, and understanding will help. This is also true of other infirmities.

The Bible teaches that the Holy Spirit will purify the heart, but the Christian must work on his own life. James makes this very clear. He teaches that the heart must be purified. "Purify your hearts, ye double minded" (Jas. 4:8). But at the same time, he teaches the human requirements of resisting the devil, drawing near to God, humbling ourselves, speaking no evil, trusting God, and rejoicing. What we know, that we should do (cf. vv. 7-17).

The Christian knows the attitude and the general direction that he should take. He knows the evil that he should shun. There are times, however, when the most dedicated saint will not know the specific will of God. This is no sin. It is only human. In no place does the Bible teach that a Christian can know all the will of God for his life in every detail.

The Bible does, however, teach that all Christians can expect divine guidance in times of uncertainties. "And I will bring the *blind* by a way that they *knew not;* I will lead them in paths that they have *not known:* I will make *darkness* light before them, and *crooked* things straight. These things will I do unto them, and not forsake them" (Isa.

42:16). A confused Christian is referred to as "blind." That is, he does not know where he is or where he is going. He is also referred to as uninformed; "knew not," a state of confusion. The path the Christian travels is described as "crooked," uncertain and dangerous. However, there is no tone of condemnation. There is evidently no sin in not always knowing the will of God, in being fearful, or in being confused. This is only human.

There is always danger that some will feel themselves an exception to any general rule. Paul seemed to recognize that some Christians would assume they had arrived at the pinnacle of all grace and would see themselves as having no need to grow. Or some Christians would think that only those in special circumstances such as ministers, young Christians, or those afflicted need to work at perfecting holiness. To try to prevent this error in understanding, Paul wrote, "Dearly beloved, let us cleanse ourselves . . . perfecting holiness" (2 Cor. 7:1). This includes Paul and all of us. The blood of Jesus Christ does cleanse from all sin; but there is no one, Paul included, who does not have room for growth and development in Christian living.

When Paul thus writes of cleansing from all filthiness of the flesh and spirit and perfecting holiness, he means that there is no place for unrighteousness of the flesh *or* spirit. If a Christian at any time, given new light by the Holy Spirit, should realize that there is anything in his life not in harmony with the will of God, that Christian *must* rid himself of that uncleanness.

Peter was prejudiced against the Gentiles' receiving the gospel; but when the Holy Spirit made it clear that they should receive the gospel, he obeyed. Here Peter freed himself from filthiness of the spirit. Because of the new light, he had added obligation. Had he refused to walk in this light, he would have sinned and faded from the pages of the Bible.

This does not mean that he would never have a battle with this problem again. The devil knows the weaknesses in our background. He will attack repeatedly. Peter had later problems concerning the Gentiles (see Gal. 2:12).

This writer has heard many Christians testify that after having walked with Christ for years they received new light that condemned some of their ways of living. They gave up these condemned ways. This is perfecting holiness.

Receiving new light, living better, knowing more about Christ, is the normal for the sanctified. As long as Christians are in these bodies, all will suffer from the infirmities of the flesh. "And not only they, but ourselves also, which have the firstfruits of the Spirit, even we ourselves groan within ourselves, waiting for the adoption, to wit, the redemption of our body" (Rom. 8:23).

The sanctified are delivered from all acts of sin and are cleansed from the carnal nature. However, all of the family of God, Paul included, await the redemption of the body from its infirmities, which will occur with glorification.

As long as the Church Militant is in this world, its members will suffer from sickness, imperfect patience, faulty thinking, and physical fatigue. These things are not sin, but neither do they make us stronger soldiers of the Cross. They hinder the Christian witness, hinder the Church, and are a stumbling block to immature Christians and to the world. Even so, infirmities are human and not sin. They cause the Church to groan and are a source of humiliation to the family of God, but they do not separate us from His grace.

The Christian does not glory in his shortcomings. Children of God enjoy the firstfruits of the Spirit, which means a knowledge of being His and assurance of redemption from sin, yet still we "groan within ourselves, waiting for the adoption, to wit, the redemption of our body" (Rom. 8:23). The word *groan* denotes "anguish and strong desire." The cry of Paul is for the complete recovery of the body from the scars of sin. This will take place only on the resurrection day.

It is important at this point to recognize the difference in a scar from sin and the sin that occasioned the scar. The scar is not guilt; it is not sin. While the scars will remain, we do not glory in them.

The body, and all nature, suffer from the Fall. All of nature, including our bodies, bears the scars of sin; but, as pointed out above, the scars are not sinful. Nature cannot sin, and neither can the body sin apart from an act of the mind. No corpse can sin. No rock or tree can sin; neither can these be filled with the Holy Spirit. Only man, who can know the will of God, who is capable of obeying or rebelling, who can serve God in holiness or sink into iniquity, can sin or be holy. However, even those who choose the way of holiness are deeply conscious of infirmities. It is true that the Christian has joy, but it is also true that the saints suffer humiliation because of their infirmities.

The child of God will do all that he knows to do to live at peace with all men. James tells us, however, that we are subject to offending (Jas. 3:2). The word *offend* means "to trip or to stumble." There are times when the child of God seeks to be a blessing but errs and hurts. One may seek to bear a burden but may do just the opposite—add to someone's burden. This should cause the Christian to groan, pray, and seek improvement in his life; but he has not sinned. The Christian must seek to keep his tongue and all members of his body in subjection to a sanctified heart, but he is kept free from sin as long as he walks in the light and obeys the known will of God.

Paul recognized the perfection of God's work in the life of man and at the same time he recognized the imperfection of humanity. "But we have this treasure in earthen vessels, that the excellency of the power may be of God, and not of us" (2 Cor. 4:7). The Spirit-filled rejoice that God the Holy Spirit would condescend to fill vessels so imperfect. The knowledge of so great a treasure serves to intensify the yearning of the saint for a more perfect manifestation of Christ in his life.

Not only does the Bible recognize the need for perfecting holiness, but the experiences of the saints testify to such a need.

Experience and Perfecting Holiness

The Bible teaches three crisis experiences: conversion, sanctification, and glorification. There is growth connected with each experience. Before one is saved, there must be a growing conviction of need. It is the deepening of this conscious need that ultimately leads one to Christ. After one is saved, there is a growing consciousness of a need for a deeper experience of the infilling of the Holy Spirit. When one is sanctified wholly, there should be a more rapid growth in grace. Growth in grace is merely perfecting our Christian experience, which is in essence perfecting holiness. On the day of resurrection our bodies will be glorified, and there will be an eternity in which, through growth, we can become more and more like Him.

The gifts of the Holy Spirit belong to the sanctified at the moment of cleansing and infilling of the Spirit. These are gifts and, as such, come instantaneously. But this does not preclude their improvement and development. The improvement of these gifts requires human cooperation with the Holy Spirit. One called to preach will be endowed with the ability to preach, but Paul advised Timothy to study, so that he could be an acceptable worker. Timothy had to cooperate with God.

41

The converted Christian becomes a child of God with a history. Truly, he is a new creature in Christ. However, he brings with him family background, attitudes, patterns of thinking, an emotional disposition, preconceived ideas, habits, personal methods of problem solving, and a set of values. When he is converted and even filled with the Holy Spirit, all of these are not changed. All sins are forgiven. He is filled with the Holy Spirit. His heart is made perfect in love, but he is still human. There is much growth needed.

As far as the human is concerned, changes will not come easily. Behavioral scientists teach us that our attitudes, self-concept, and problem-solving methods are relatively permanent. In fact, the change that is normal is to become more of what we are. Within man's own powers, the outlook for meaningful change is dim. God will change our lives. Man can be born again. However, the sanctified soon learn that they are still very much human. Their genetic human nature and their cultural patterns are still the same. Paul, Peter, and all followers of Christ must learn, grow, and discipline their lives.

The Christian will not have been saved and sanctified for very long before he will recognize great need for maturity. In the light of human experience and scriptural teachings, how unwise for the professed Christian to excuse, rationalize, and drift on, seemingly giving no heed to the voice of the Holy Spirit as He speaks, seeks to teach and pinpoint faults, shortcomings, and other human frailties that are hindrances to spiritual growth! When the Holy Spirit calls a halt, man should stop; when He speaks, man should listen; when He reveals, man should walk in the light.

These are the times that the sanctified may meet their most severe temptations. At the time of one's sanctification, his all, including present and future, is given to God.

"I beseech you therefore, brethren, by the mercies of God, that ye present your bodies a living sacrifice, holy, acceptable unto God, which is your reasonable service" (Rom. 12:1). Satan does not give up because one's consecration has been made. Satan may well contest the sanctified one's walking in new light. The saint may be tempted toward carelessness. Such occasions are critical, for light rejected will become an occasion for sin.

Some sanctified people seem to think that when they were sanctified the day of decision-making was over. Not so! It is true that the carnal nature was eradicated and the heart was filled with the Holy Spirit. But the Spirit-filled soon learn that there is a need for self-control, discipline, and spiritual care. Spiritual peril encircles the sanctified throughout his life. There is need for self-control over the thought life, attitudes, talking, and every other aspect of life. There is no sin in temptation so long as invitation to sin is rejected. Temptation is a reminder that the Christian life requires vigilance.

No sanctified person will ever cease to marvel that God would be willing to fill his life with His presence. He realizes that it is not sinful to be human, but a glorious privilege. There is the joy of knowing that now one's life is free from sin and fully possessed by God.

Along with the consciousness of freedom from all sin comes the realization that scars from sin are still there. The attitude of the sanctified, as has been pointed out, is very important at this stage. He must not glory in his indulgence. Human weaknesses do not require forgiveness, but they should be worked on. The Christian who loves God with all his heart will seek to improve, overcome, and minimize error and infirmities in his life.

The Holy Spirit seeks to make common cause with Christians in their effort to be victorious over infirmities. In all human weaknesses and perplexities, He understands with perfect understanding. At such times He comes, not to condemn, but with compassion and love that seeks to help. In all human weaknesses, He is there to give strength.

The saints of God are conscious of mistakes, spiritual ignorance, and the frustration of perfect motives by imperfect perception. They must resist the temptation to become careless and excuse failure with the alibi that this is just human nature.

Indifference toward perfecting holiness is not the spirit of perfect love. Indifference toward spiritual growth may become contempt for the known will of God. With this attitude there is danger of using human nature as an excuse to hold on to pet sins. This cannot be a Christian's attitude. For the sanctified, the rule is positive: Obey God!

The child of God is not condemned as a sinner when the Holy Spirit sheds new light into his life and he realizes that he falls short of God's will and that there are new things to do and some things to give up. There comes that moment when the will of God is made known. *This is critical!* Those who continue to walk in the light remain free from sin. If there is rebellion, there is sin.

Every Christian by the help of the Holy Spirit can walk in the light, shun evil, and walk in the highway of holiness. Through carelessness and indifference one may drift away from God. He may become enslaved again by physical appetites. The Christian must mortify the flesh. He must not yield to self-indulgence. Paul's advice to the church is clear: "Set your affection on things above, not on things on the earth. . . . Mortify therefore your members which are upon the earth; fornication, uncleanness, inordinate affection, evil concupiscence, and covetousness, which is idolatry" (Col. 3:2, 5).

The Spirit-filled remembers well when he died to the world of sin and self. As things of the world passed away, the things which belong to the spiritual life became more important. The object of his longing is to be more like Christ.

The life of the sanctified is not one of drifting into heaven, but one of strenuous endeavor and active service. There must be strength of will to dismiss from the thought life that which is worldly. The sanctified not only die to actual sin but to that which is questionable, even the very taint of sin.

The whole bent of thought and disposition is to serve God in holiness. Things of this earth that are not within themselves sinful must be kept in a secondary place, lest they lead to evil through being preferred to things that are spiritual. Things of the world are of small concern to the sanctified. This is true because he is dead to the world.

The sanctified live as those who have been made perfect in love but are seeking to be more and more like Christ. There is perfection, but there is also growth in perfection. That is, there is perfection in that one is made perfect in love; but beyond this, there is growth in the exemplification of perfect love. For instance, a newly sanctified man may be naturally gruff. He needs to work on this infirmity, so that others may see the perfect love behind the gruffness.

The sanctified Christian has need of daily growth in seeking to rid himself of errors and shortcomings. Perfect motives from a heart made pure do not insure perfect understanding or action. There are errors in one's life of which the sanctified have no knowledge, even when others may see. These infirmities need the blood of Jesus Christ, but they are not sins of guilt. They also need the understanding of other Christians. Because of God's perfect understanding of the Christian's motive life, the saint may be holy in the sight of God even when men may misunderstand and the Christian groans within himself.

It is human to err. Some mistakes are unavoidable. It

is the privilege of every child of God to seek the help of the Holy Spirit. "Likewise the Spirit also helpeth our infirmities" (Rom. 8:26). Even though infirmities may cause the Christian to feel humble and unworthy, the glory of it is that all the redeemed are the children of God. The hope of the Christian is not in his humanity but in a life filled with the Holy Spirit. In Him the weak can be strong. Within himself the Christian can do nothing.

SUMMARY

The sanctified will seek daily to perfect his Christian life. He enjoys the assurance of all sins forgiven and heart made pure, but there is the realization that, for the love of the Heavenly Father, he should work endlessly to make his life as Christlike in action as possible. The Christian is motivated toward perfecting holiness, not through fear of guilt, but by love and by a desire to more perfectly express the love that God has given to him.

The Scriptures are very clear in their teachings concerning the responsibility of the individual Christian to perfect his own Christian life, "perfecting holiness in the fear of God" (2 Cor. 7:1). The motive given for this perfecting of holiness is "the fear of God." Infirmities—meaning mental and physical weaknesses—are all a part of human nature and not inherently evil. We work to overcome these to be better Christians.

The Christian's daily problems teach him the need to perfect his experience. He will find, however, that changes of speech, attitudes, and cultural behavior come slowly. All men are a part of their past history and their genetic inheritance.

Chapter 4

The Human Factor

Spirit-filled Christians are fully equipped to serve God. Such followers of Christ have been saved from sin, purified, and filled with the Holy Spirit. It would be a dangerous error, however, for anyone to expect that these experiences bring one to a religious state so perfect that a life of holiness would be automatic with no human effort needed.

It is true that the Holy Spirit brings power to one's life, but the Bible requires each sanctified person to conform to holy living with a diligence that cannot be compromised. The Church is taught, "Follow peace with all men, and holiness, without which no man shall see the Lord" (Heb. 12:14). In this verse there is teaching with a warning. Christians are to seek peace with all men but not to the point of compromising the requirements of holiness. Holy living must come first. For the sanctified, living a holy life is a way of following the Lord with all diligence. The duty is twofold: seek to be at peace with all men but, first, be fully dedicated to living a holy life without compromise.

Being sanctified is only the beginning, for there is a life to be lived. The Bible makes this clear. "The God of peace . . . make you perfect in every good work to do his will" (Heb. 13:20-21) is the writer's prayer for his Christian readers. Here the word *perfect* means "to integrate one's powers" or "the harmonious combination of powers to function together in the achieving of the divine will." The Holy Spirit endues us with power to do the will of God. Now it is up to us to use sanctified faculties to serve the Lord.

Being made perfect does not dehumanize us. Man's infirmities are always with him. However, for the Spirit-filled, each act is both an act of the Holy Spirit *and* an act of man. God the Holy Spirit works within us, and in Him our human weaknesses are made strong.

Human nature is such that it will err even when enjoying the marvel of being filled with the Spirit. However, man is helped by receiving guidance, checks, warnings, additional light, and deeper insight concerning the things of God. Through human cooperation with such divine help holiness is perfected. "Having therefore these promises, dearly beloved, let us cleanse ourselves from all filthiness of the flesh and spirit, perfecting holiness in the fear of God" (2 Cor. 7:1).

If holiness is to be perfected, Christians must separate from associates, things, and places that would tend to defile their lives. For some it has meant giving up job, family, and friends. The Scriptures express this positively: "Abstain from all appearance of evil" (1 Thess. 5:22).

There are two major ways by which one may perfect holiness: through discipline and through maturity.

PERFECTING HOLINESS THROUGH DISCIPLINE

The Christian must have the necessary spiritual power to do what he knows to be right and he must have the needed self-control to resist what is evil or even questionable. His love for God must be master of natural appetites.

A dedication to God that will motivate one to seek to do His will with all of one's heart is the source of Christian discipline. God will help us to do His will and reject evil, but there is much that we must do. Paul was careful not to permit the physical to gain the upper hand. "But I keep under my body, and bring it into subjection: lest that by any means, when I have preached to others, I myself should be a castaway" (1 Cor. 9:27).

Paul is not teaching that the body is sinful. He is teaching that the body must be controlled. The spiritual man must be master of all appetites which arise from the flesh. All natural and normal appetites are servants of the Christian, and the spiritual man is not a slave of his appetites.

The physical discipline Paul found necessary for the prosecution of God's work was so severe that he expressed it as if he were a fighter beating and bruising his body. Paul was master, and his body was a slave doing the will of the Spirit. Paul's life was one directed by the Holy Spirit with full cooperation of the human spirit, his body playing the part of a slave.

While Paul never accused the body of being inherently sinful, he did recognize that the body could become a source of trouble to the spiritual life. There must be a spirit of self-denial and abstinence from self-indulgence. The undisciplined body is an adversary of the spirit.

There is no innate sin in any natural appetite, but there is potential sin in any unbridled desire. In 1 Corinthians 9, Paul's mind is fixed on winning the race and gaining heaven. He perceives the greatest hindrance to this goal to be his own appetites if they are not restrained.

Paul tells the way of victory. "This I say then, Walk in the Spirit, and ye shall not fulfil the lust of the flesh" (Gal. 5:16). Paul is telling men that their lives should be regulated by the Spirit. The sanctified should conduct themselves by always walking in the Spirit. In no way is Paul teaching that the body is evil. He is teaching that within man are inherent drives that if left undisciplined will become the seat of evil.

One may have his heart purified by the Holy Spirit, but temptation is still as real as it was to Adam, Eve, and Jesus. Being tempted through physical needs does not make the physical evil. Jesus had a physical body and was tempted, but He was sinless. "For we have not an high priest which cannot be touched with the feeling of our infirmities; but was in all points tempted like as we are, yet without sin" (Heb. 4:15). "For such an high priest became us, who is holy, harmless, undefiled, separate from sinners, and made higher than the heavens" (Heb. 7:26).

The Spirit-filled are freed from the carnal nature, but Paul places a requirement for discipline and aggressive spiritual living on every Christian.

It takes discipline to keep the sanctified mind free from worldly thoughts and centered on spiritual values. Paul tells the Church to bring "into captivity every thought to the obedience of Christ" (2 Cor. 10:5). The Christian will fight temptation at this point.

This is especially important for young Christians. The Christian is reminded that he does not fight these battles unaided. "For the weapons of our warfare are not carnal, but mighty through God to the pulling down of strong holds" (2 Cor. 10:4). Here again, the need for Christian discipline is taught. The Holy Spirit will make the Spirit-filled strong, but the battle is "our warfare." The sanctified can conquer all the fortresses of the flesh and the devil through the power of the Holy Spirit.

The Christian can be so completely victorious that his following Christ is seen as perfect in the sight of God. The saint is still human with all his physical attributes, but his life and work can be fully accepted before a holy God, for it is God who works in the Spirit-filled to "make you perfect in every good work to do his will, working in you that which is wellpleasing in his sight, through Jesus Christ; to whom be glory for ever and ever" (Heb. 13:21).

In order to obey the commands of God and his own conscience the Christian must internalize the truths taught in the Bible and by his church. He will enjoy self-control, not because of reward and punishment (these have a place), but because of his personal faith. The boundaries set by his beliefs make his path clear, and he knows where he stands on particular issues. If he is approaching an issue, he knows it. If it is questionable, out of his love for God, he will turn from evil. External control is limited in its effect, but the internal control that comes from accepting the Bible and the rules of one's church as a code of conduct is a discipline that brings its reward in a clear conscience and full acceptance before God. Conscience and motives are learned and must be developed.

The young Christian starts his Christian life almost completely dependent upon Christian teachers for doctrines and standards of conduct. Yet the babe in Christ must have some freedom, but not license, to develop his faith. If one is to become an autonomous adult Christian, there must be Bible-based conviction that he has fully accepted as his guide for living.

Christian discipline is learned best in a sound, Bible-based, Spirit-anointed, divine-love-motivated church. The spiritual climate is as important as the truth that is taught. Educational experts learned long ago that children and adults learn faster and better in an atmosphere where they feel fully accepted.

The young Christian will develop his faith and discipline best when he is taught discipline with Christian dignity. The ideals and principles taught must be scrip-

51

tural. No longer do people accept truths just because the minister or church says they are so.

When Bible-centered truth is taught under the power of the Holy Spirit and the Christian accepts this truth as the faith by which he will live, there will be the best kind of discipline—Christian self-discipline. Such a Christian has his values, code, and goals; and he knows why he has accepted them. He will resist all evil, and he will seek all good. He realizes and accepts the fact that there is much for which he is responsible in Christian living. Christian duty will be carried out, not through fear, but motivated through love for God, his church, and the Christian way.

PERFECTING HOLINESS THROUGH MATURITY

For the purpose of clarity, think of a mature person as one who is able to face life's realities, make necessary decisions, and accept the responsibility for his decisions. The mature person is able to accept others into his world, feel with others, share their joys and sorrows; but he will not lose himself in others. He will retain his own values, faith, and integrity. The mature person has had experiences, has thought through some of life's questions, and has studied and accepted some beliefs and rejected some ideas. He has a set of values and a code of conduct he will not compromise. He is not easily shaken. He is not too rigid to listen, but he is too strong to be easily moved by questions and will not give up his beliefs.

Paul seemed to have this in mind when he wrote, "That ye be not soon shaken in mind, or be troubled, neither by spirit, nor by word, nor by letter as from us, as that the day of Christ is at hand" (2 Thess. 2:2). The Apostle Paul seemed puzzled. It was such a short time before that he had taught the church at Thessalonica truths concerning the second coming of Christ, but now they were confused. Paul's point is that they should not be confused even if a letter came with his own name signed to it.

Mature people know their goals and how they expect to reach them. This takes time. The attainment of Christian maturity takes place gradually. It is a growth process following the experiences of conversion and sanctification, wherein the Christian makes progress in his ability to be more Christlike. Not all Christians progress at the same pace.

Paul speaks of our growing in Christlikeness. "But speaking the truth in love, may grow up into him in all things, which is the head, even Christ" (Eph. 4:15).

If the Christian is given a stable spiritual church home, he can be expected to progress toward normal Christian maturity with a minimum amount of difficulty. Apart from the initial experiences of conversion and sanctification, there is no more important duty for the Christian than that of pressing toward the prize of spiritual maturity. "As newborn babes, desire the sincere milk of the word, that ye may grow thereby" (1 Pet. 2:2). The Greek word for *desire* means "intense yearning." So strong is the Christian desire for God's truth and growth that it becomes first among all desires. Surely, this would mean that the maturing Christian puts God first in all things at all times.

It is an accepted premise in psychology that, all things being equal, a child reared in a home where there is genuine love has a solid foundation for the development of a healthy emotional life. In the same light, one may safely assume that when one truly places God first in his life he has a solid foundation for the development of a healthy spiritual life.

For the purpose of clarity of understanding, let us analyze four characteristics of spiritual maturity.

53

1. *An understanding heart.* "Give therefore thy servant an understanding heart to judge thy people, that I may discern between good and bad: for who is able to judge this thy so great a people?" (1 Kings 3:9). Solomon is asking for a "hearing heart." Literally, he is asking God to give him intelligence: but, even more, he is asking that he shall have the capacity to hear with feeling. This pleased God, who answered, "Behold I have done according to thy words" (1 Kings 3:12).

A mature person is tolerant and discerning with himself and others. There is a growing understanding of his own feelings and a better understanding of the feelings and actions of others.

With this understanding, there comes satisfaction in daily tasks. The mature do not depend upon public rewards, but find their reward in an inward assurance that they have done their assigned task and have done it well. The inward, or intrinsic, reward is the most important reward.

The understanding heart feels and thinks in a world of reality. There is no depreciation of self or others. This kind of Christian is an insightful person. He avoids assigning meaning and motives to the actions of others.

The understanding person is flexible. This flexibility of personality helps one make necessary adjustments. Understanding brings new light, and new light requires new adjustment. How easy it is to misunderstand someone! How often one finds that his conclusions were in error, and then how necessary for one to readjust his thinking to this new knowledge!

It is immature and neurotic to be hard or unyielding in all things. This does not mean that the mature have no roots and that they change with every wind. They do not. In fact, their spiritual roots resist the wind. It does mean that they reject the darkness of ignorance and al-

54

ways grow toward the light, a type of spiritual phototropism.

2. *Long-suffering.* A child's nature, which is immature, demands that his needs be met immediately or he will sound forth his displeasure. The mature person can fully realize his need, but he is able to postpone satisfaction when necessary. He does not live for the now. The mature person has the ability to establish future goals and values. Such a person can deny himself, take up his cross, and do it without undue complaint.

The mature Christian is tolerant of those who are different. This does not mean that he enjoys, approves, or accepts what the other person does, but he does not reject the person. The roots of his own personal faith are so deep and well established that people who are different do not make him fearful.

Paul gives us some insight into this mature spiritual state in Col. 1:10-11: "Increasing in the knowledge of God; strengthened with all might . . . unto all patience and long-suffering with joyfulness." The word "walk" refers to one's behavior. Paul says that if the Christian will earnestly put into practice all that he knows he will arrive at the position of having patience and long-suffering with joy.

We often refer to the "patience of Job." The truth is that Job endured with great spiritual struggle. Even so, he was "a perfect and an upright man" (Job 1:8). Spiritual maturity has much to do with the calmness and gentleness with which one suffers.

3. *Acceptance.* One may have an understanding heart, be long-suffering, and still fall short of what a mature Christian should be. The mature child of God becomes involved. "Bear ye one another's burdens, and so fulfil the law of Christ" (Gal. 6:2). A child lives in a world of self. His personal needs constitute his world. As he matures, he includes his family, city, state, nation, and

55

world. The mature Christian reaches to the world. He cares for the Church and for the fallen. There is a concern for the strong and for those who are weak. In a state of mind that seeks to restore and not punish, he reaches out to those in need. He can do this only when he accepts them.

Again, this is not to be understood that one approves of a person's failings. The mature Christian accepts the fact that people do unpleasant things, but they are still to be loved. They are loved for themselves, not for what they have done.

All Christians will prefer the company of some more than others. This is true because all people are not alike; therefore, some appeal to us more than do others. This is human. But a Christian must not reject those who are not of his inner circle. "And he took with him Peter and the two sons of Zebedee, and began to be sorrowful and very heavy" (Matt. 26:37). In His hour of great sorrow Jesus took Peter, James, and John farther than the others. But He did not reject the other disciples. The mature Christian does not exclude people from his fellowship just because they are different.

The mature Christian not only accepts people, but he has accepted a creed by which he lives. He knows what is expected of him by his church, and he is willing to accept this. He is dependable.

The acceptance of God, self, others, and one's responsibility contribute to mature Christian living.

4. *Regard.* "Then Peter opened his mouth, and said, Of a truth I perceive that God is no respecter of persons" (Acts 10:34). The person who walks with the Lord will become more and more like Him. This includes a deep and sincere regard for himself and others. This is not to deny

that one has negative characteristics; even so, he does not reject himself. The person who despises or continually criticizes himself is spiritually immature. Only when a person has love for himself will he be able to highly regard others.

Regard for self and for others must be sincere. In the quiet of one's own private world, suffering over errors and other infirmities of the flesh, there is still regard for oneself as an immortal being. This regard for self and for others should be a growing experience.

SUMMARY

The Spirit-filled Christian is equipped to perfect holiness, but this does not come about automatically. He must strive to conform to holy living with uncompromising diligence, a diligence that is demanding physically, mentally, and spiritually. The Holy Spirit, however, aids every effort.

There are two major ways in which one perfects holiness: through discipline and through maturity. Discipline involves the subjection of the body to the spiritual. The body is not sinful, but it can be an occasion for sin. Temptation is still real for the sanctified. The mind, also, must be disciplined. While the mind is not evil, thoughts can be evil. The right church environment is indispensable to developing proper discipline.

Holiness is also perfected through maturity, which is attained gradually and at different rates by different people. Again, a nourishing church environment is invaluable. There are at least four characteristics of Christian maturity: (1) *An understanding heart*—with which the Christian understands himself and others; (2) *Long-suffering*—a characteristic that makes it possible to postpone satisfactions, plan for the future, deny self, and show tolerance for those who are different to oneself; (3) *Acceptance*—of self and others even when there are shortcomings, and acceptance of a creed by which one lives; and (4) *Regard*—for self and others.

Chapter 5

Development in Holiness

Every Christian is faced with certain developmental tasks. These are tasks that are imposed on one through the need for spiritual growth at specific periods in life. The demands for such development come from the Bible, the Holy Spirit, and the Christian community.

Specific tasks should never be demanded until the Christian is strong enough and spiritually adult enough to understand and accept his developmental needs. Men may try to rush growth, but God never does. Pushing the young Christian before his time of readiness will only cause confusion and could cause defeat. The church must work carefully with the Holy Spirit and lead the young Christian slowly from one developmental task to the next, not faster than he is able to progress, but step by step as he is able to gain from each experience.

Only when one is spiritually motivated will he profit from each new developmental task. "And the child grew, and waxed strong in spirit, and was in the deserts till the day of his shewing unto Israel" (Luke 1:80). This scripture refers to John the Baptist, a man filled with the Holy Spirit and destined to prepare the way for Christ. "He shall be great in the sight of the Lord, and shall drink neither wine nor strong drink; and he shall be filled with the Holy Ghost, even from his mother's womb" (Luke 1:15). Even with the prophecy that he was to be great in the sight of God and filled with the Holy Ghost, John did not begin his work until he "was strong in spirit." A spiritual child should not be rushed forth to do the work of a mature spiritual warrior.

DEVELOPMENTAL TASKS

Following are some of the primary developmental tasks.

1. *Walk on your own.* Christians are expected to learn to walk alone to some degree. This does not mean that church members will not bear one another's burdens. It does mean that no Christian will live all of his life leaning on others.

The New Testament perceived the maturing Christian as one who is able to take solid food. "But strong meat belongeth to them that are of full age, even those who by reason of use have their senses exercised to discern both good and evil" (Heb. 5:14). The type of Christian here described does not have to be spoon-fed by others. He is able to read the Bible, believe God's Word, accept the truth, and walk in God's will for his own life. This comes by growth and is not an instantaneous achievement.

2. *Become stable.* Christian stability is learned. The person who is stable in most other areas of his life is more apt to be stable in his Christian life.

All Christians can achieve some degree of stability. This may be done through systematic Bible study and the study of choice Christian literature with a major emphasis on Christian doctrine. The pastor can contribute through doctrinal preaching. Paul was emphasizing this need of knowing why we hold a belief when he wrote, "That we henceforth be no more children, tossed to and fro, and carried about with every wind of doctrine, by the sleight of men, and cunning craftiness, whereby they lie in wait to deceive" (Eph. 4:14).

3. **Relate to others.** Learning to relate oneself spiritually to others is a major factor in one's enjoyment of church life. Even in the church one must not be too demanding, inflexible, and vocal. Respect for others and self requires a calm dignity in all relations. "And let us consider one another to provoke unto love and to good works" (Heb. 10:24).

4. **Develop a good conscience.** The development of a Christian conscience is a task of major importance. One's background and present environment are of significance. If one is to be a happy Christian, he must be able to distinguish right from wrong without too much struggle or guilt feelings.

It is well to keep in mind at all times that past teachings cannot be separated from present feelings of freedom or guilt. The conscience must be Bible-based. That is, the Christian is guided in his conduct by the teachings of God's Word.

Another area for help is found in the rules of one's church. These rules reflect the general conscience of the denominational membership over a period of many years.

A third source of guidance in the development of the conscience is the direct teaching of the Holy Spirit. He will not teach us to be too different from the other children of God. As a loving Companion, He will lead gently and carefully. He will never be harsh or unkind in giving directions. His guidance brings understanding and stability to our lives, never confusion and vacillation.

In psychology, it is considered a mark of emotional illness if a person frequently swings to opposite extremes in his feelings. In a spiritual sense this is true with one's conscience. If a person is swayed by every difference of opinion in sermon, song, book, or testimony, he is spiritually unhealthy.

The cure for such instability is found in relying on God and learning from the right people. "In all thy ways acknowledge him, and he shall direct thy paths" (Prov. 3:6). The cure will not come rapidly. If you were reared in a stern, harsh, or unkind home, you will find it hard to arrive at a spiritual maturity that will not consciously or unconsciously make you feel that God, our Father, is stern, harsh, or unkind. Time will help, but one's past experiences with undue severity will always be a problem.

An inadequate conscience is also a problem for some. They may be at the altar over and over for something that they have done. They find it hard to be loyal to the church. They show marked spiritual immaturity, are irresponsible, and have poor judgment. It is obvious that the first need of such a person is to be sure that he is saved and filled with the Spirit of God.

The inadequate conscience is a special problem of the teen years. Adolescents are "becoming" persons, and they have much social and spiritual learning to do. How well and how fast they learn will depend much upon their backgrounds and their present environments. If they come from cold, unemotional homes filled with parental conflict, erratic punishment, and neglect, the development of a healthy conscience will be slow. Fellow church members will need an abundance of divine grace to be patient, forgiving, and, above all, spiritual models for the immature Christian. For many young Christians, the development of a healthy conscience requires a complete reeducation. The major need for their growth is a church of Spirit-filled members who serve as mature models.

5. *Adopt sound attitudes.* Attitudes are learned. The development of wholesome attitudes is necessary, for they are relatively permanent. A religious experience does not

eradicate all unwholesome attitudes in a moment's time. There is some work to be done on the part of the individual.

An attitude is a set response to persons, situations, or ideas. Attitudes are learned largely in the home and from one's peer group. Often the person is not conscious of having particular attitudes, and therefore the attitudes are unrecognized. This makes the person psychologically complex. In many attitudes the emotions play a more dynamic role than the intellect. Attitudes once acquired resist modification.

We have already seen that Paul felt strongly that Peter's attitude toward the Gentiles was wrong. "But when Peter was come to Antioch, I withstood him to the face, because he was to be blamed. For before that certain came from James, he did eat with the Gentiles: but when they were come, he withdrew and separated himself, fearing them which were of the circumcision" (Gal. 2:11-12).

All his life Peter had been taught that he should not eat with persons of another nation. After Peter had been saved and filled with the Spirit, God gave him a vision that forced him to admit that the Gentiles were not unclean. He did preach to the Gentiles and did eat with them, as is recorded in Acts 10. When some of the Church demanded that the Gentiles accept circumcision and keep the law of Moses, the apostles and elders called a meeting to consider the matter. "And when there had been much disputing, Peter rose up, and said unto them, Men and brethren, ye know how that a good while ago God made choice among us, that the Gentiles by my mouth should hear the word of the gospel, and believe. And God, which knoweth the hearts, bare them witness, giving them the Holy Ghost, even as he did unto us; and put no difference between us and them, purifying their hearts by faith" (Acts 15:7-9). Here Peter stood like a rock, undaunted and unmoved. How noble he was in this hour of victory to be so human and weak later when Paul had to face him because he refused to eat with the Gentiles! Fear of people was the occasion for his retreat to old attitudes and conduct. But Peter was still a Christian, apostle, and child of God. In fact, Paul records the entire story to show that he is Peter's equal as an apostle. Paul in no way questioned Peter's Christian experience.

6. *Develop responsible behavior patterns.* Achieving mature behavior is desirable and necessary. Immature conduct is no compliment to the Christian. "When I was a child, I spake as a child, I understood as a child, I thought as a child: but when I became a man, I put away childish things" (1 Cor. 13:11).

Paul is not writing about giving up sin. That had already been done. The admonition here is to grow. "We are bound to thank God always for you, brethren, as it is meet, because that your faith groweth exceedingly, and the charity of every one of you all toward each other aboundeth" (2 Thess. 1:3).

Even though Paul is mature and has put away childish things, he confesses that there are many things that he does not know and that life holds riddles for him. "For now we see through a glass, darkly [life is seen as a riddle]; but then face to face: now I know in part; but then shall I know even as also I am known" (1 Cor. 13:12). He sees things obscurely and imperfectly.

Achieving responsible behavior is a lifelong task that will be fully realized only when we get to heaven. We learn what responsible behavior is from spiritual adult Christians, the Bible, and the personal guidance of the Holy Spirit. The mature Christian should be an example to the immature Christian. The spiritual child should read his Bible, for this is the Book of Life. The Holy Spirit does give guidance for those who seek it.

There are times when the Holy Spirit leads through

the Scriptures, mature Christians, and through special checks or promptings. However, in reading the Scriptures one will find that, although the Lord did work a miracle on the road to Damascus to bring Saul to his conversion (Acts 9), this was an exceptional act and not one to be repeated. Following this miracle, the Lord used mature Christians such as Ananias (Acts 9:10), the disciples (Acts 9:26), and Barnabas (Acts 9:27) to carry on Saul's spiritual education.

Truly Paul was guided by the Holy Spirit, but even here the Lord used men. "As they ministered to the Lord, and fasted, the Holy Ghost said, Separate me Barnabas and Saul for the work whereunto I have called them. And when they had fasted and prayed, and laid their hands on them, they sent them away" (Acts 13:2-3). Paul was filled with the Holy Ghost to give him the power to do the will of God. However, Paul was taught, instructed, and advised by the mature Christians in the church.

There are times when God's guidance is as the sound of thunder; but most of life's guidance is the quiet, patient, tender movement of the Spirit through the Bible and the church. Most of life's guidance in achieving mature behavior will be God's use of His Word and His called servants.

Young Christians who are seeking guidance by voices from heaven, visions, or other conspicuous manifestations are not being scriptural. God can give such guidance, but a study of the Scriptures will show that this is seldom done. Walking in the light as He leads and being true to light given will lead one safely through this life to the perfection of glorification in the world to come.

Development does not come about without effort on the part of the Christian. One must be willing to help himself. In counseling, it is an accepted principle that the client cannot be helped unless he desires to be helped.

This desire must be manifested by the client's willingness to face reality, accept the fact that he has a need, consider possible alternatives of action, make a decision, do some planning, and carry out the plans. Only when these steps are taken will there be healthy mental and emotional growth. The same may be applied to spiritual growth.

EVASION OF GROWTH

Man's nature is such that he cannot long tolerate disequilibrium. If trouble, demands, or fears cause tension, the human organism finds this highly distressing and will seek to relieve the threat in order to return to a state of emotional poise.

In one's growth and development he will accumulate a store of partially unconscious adjustive behavior patterns. Psychologists call these defense mechanisms (because they defend from anxiety) or adjustive mechanisms. These ways of meeting life's demands are learned, and they are not, within themselves and within limits, psychologically bad or spiritually evil. In fact, these defense mechanisms are needed to resolve conflict and free the individual from unnecessary anxiety. They can, however, become a serious problem when they are overused. They may distort reality and thereby leave the problem unsolved.

The Christian can be adversely affected by the over-use of these mechanisms. In this case, the person is unconsciously dodging reality and living in a world of fiction. Such a person will remain spiritually immature and unstable.

The maturing Christian knows that he must face the demands of Christian living, make decisions, and accept the responsibilities of living with the consequences of his decisions. Even the mature Christian will find some of life's demands unpleasant, and he will be strongly tempted to evade spiritual growth by using defensive techniques. Some of those most frequently used are briefly discussed. A more complete listing from the approach of pure psychology may be found in any psychology textbook.

1. *Fantasy.* The Christian who uses fantasy goes through all the acts of being a saint in his imagination. He dreams away at prayer, Bible reading, and church faithfulness. He knows what to do, how to do it, and believes that these things should be done, but he finds it easy to tarry in his dream world. This temptation to live in a world of fantasy must be resisted. It is normal for a child to live in a play world but not for an adult.

2. *Projection.* When one is faced with painful reality and will not accept this truth, he may unconsciously try to protect his ego by finding fault with others. The Christian who does not live up to his own best ideals may claim that those who do attain these standards do it only for show. If he can pull others down to his level, he feels more at ease with his own shortcomings. Churches are filled with the spiritually immature who dissipate their spiritual energies finding fault with others. They never seem to realize that the driving motive for this attitude is their own shortcomings.

3. *Nomadism.* This spiritual defense mechanism is used by the person who wanders from church to church seeking acceptance. There is a need in his life, but that need will never be met by trying to escape by running. Move after move does not bring peace or gain, but still he seeks a contentment he does not have.

This may well be more of an emotional problem than a spiritual one. This person may live a good life other than his wandering. The best procedure for him is to talk his problem over with some minister in whom he has confidence. As he talks and explores the problem, he may find the problem is not within the church but within himself.

Blessed is the person who has a minister who will listen to his problem without giving a lecture. The person needs time to talk out his problem and explore his emotional life if he is to identify his problem. He may have a spiritual problem, but not necessarily so. Honestly facing the problem will bring out the truth.

4. *Regression.* When the pressure is on and problems come thick and fast, the Christian may feel so frustrated that he longs for and seeks the security of past blessings. In fact, all people do this to some degree at some point in life. A mild degree of regression is not bad; but when one begins to live in the past, he is no longer facing the realities of present-day needs. He will find himself forsaking the spiritual battles of today and living on the victories of yesterday.

The yesterdays may truly have been golden and wonderful, and the present may be painful and hard, but the Christian cannot regress to the past as a way of living. It is only human to remember and enjoy the past, but it is spiritually unhealthy to accept the realities of today.

5. *Rationalization.* When one feels a need to justify his conduct because he has acted impulsively and because his action is not desirable, he may try to make his actions appear reasonable and acceptable. The danger is that the person in seeking to appear "good" may not be willing to face the truth. This is the tragic road of self-deception.

If one is never elected to a church office or is never asked to accept a responsibility, he may save his self-esteem by claiming pure and noble motivation for acts that cause him to be left out. He may claim that he is too honest to be false, and therefore he says just what he thinks.

Honesty is noble, but speaking so freely without regard for others is damaging to God's kingdom. This may be overlooked for a time in a babe in Christ; but, even

68

here, the Christian must face up to his responsibility to live in a world of Christian reality, change his ways, consider others, grow up, and be a mature Christian. If not, his rationalizing and immaturity will become the occasion for sin.

There is innocence in not knowing better; but when light comes, it is to be walked in. Excuses to make oneself feel more comfortable are not compatible with the Christian life.

6. *Reaction formation.* The Christian may find himself unduly hard on someone for something that he does. This does not in any way mean that he must approve the other's action. The question is, Why does he feel so strongly? One may be critical of another for taking too active a part in church activities when the real problem is that the person who is critical would like to take part but is fearful of doing so. It is a secure and mature Christian who can honestly face himself in the full exposure of the light that God gives. When one thus faces himself, he is on the way to healthy spiritual growth.

7. *Undoing.* This is a technique whereby a person divests himself of guilt by some act that "cleanses" him from the guilt of his conduct. It may be seen in the conduct of one who is in the habit of speaking sharply and then trying to wash away the hurt with a laugh. Unconsciously he feels he can thus rid himself of the responsibility of his conduct. Such conduct may be of long standing and the person unconscious of his acts. However, the Holy Spirit is faithful to help us know ourselves, and if we are responsive to this revelation, we will begin to live and act in the real world and not in a world of our own making.

Human nature is strong and complex. There are many things in all of us of which we are unaware. Man is so constituted that his very nature seeks to protect his own private picture of himself. This is so true that to know oneself is impossible without the help of the Holy Spirit.

Powerful unconscious forces are working to defend the self-image. Such forces are not evil. In fact, they are necessary. Blessed is the man who thinks well of himself! Jesus said it differently: "Thou shalt love thy neighbour as thyself" (Matt. 19:19). Your happiness is important to you. From the scripture, this is the way that it should be. One's life, happiness, and adjustments are committed to himself.

Christian love is honest. A man who truly loves himself will be honest with himself and true to himself. The same scripture teaches that one should respect his family. "Honour thy father and thy mother." It would seem a reasonable conclusion that the person in whom such love abides will do all that he can to so live that he will reflect honor on his family and on himself as well as on his God.

Perfecting holiness through development is not a way of life that is a burden. It is a way of life that is peaceful, without pretense, and therefore mentally and spiritually healthy. What can be better than being at peace with God, self, and others?

It is in the very nature of all life to grow. The drive for growth is so strong that it is growth to maturity or it is sickness, abnormality, or death. This is true spiritually as well as physically and mentally.

SUMMARY

As the Christian grows in grace, this normal process perfects his experience of holiness. "But the path of the just is as the shining light, that shineth more and more unto the perfect day" (Prov. 4:18). Some evidence of growth is seen in the Christian's ability to walk alone (that is, show some spiritual independence), gain stability, relate to others, develop a healthy conscience, learn wholesome attitudes, and achieve mature behavior.

Some growth is painful. Man's nature rejects anything that causes anxiety. Some methods of evading the pains of growth are *fantasy,* which is living in an imaginary spiritual world; *nomadism,* which is escaping problems by running; *projection,* which is attributing one's motives to others; *regression,* which is living in the past; *rationalization,* which is justifying undesirable behavior; *reaction formation,* which is acting just the opposite to the way one feels; and *undoing,* which is trying to absolve oneself from guilt by a compensating act.

The healthy Christian will face reality, consider alternatives, make decisions, plan his actions, and accept the consequences. It takes determined effort to be a growing Christian. The Holy Spirit will help us to become more and more Christlike. Freedom from sin comes in a moment of time, but there should be a lifetime of acquiring the characteristics of Christlikeness.